DICKHEAD SERIES

Amusing Swear Words To Color

For Stress Releasing

By

Queenie McJody

Happy Coloring!

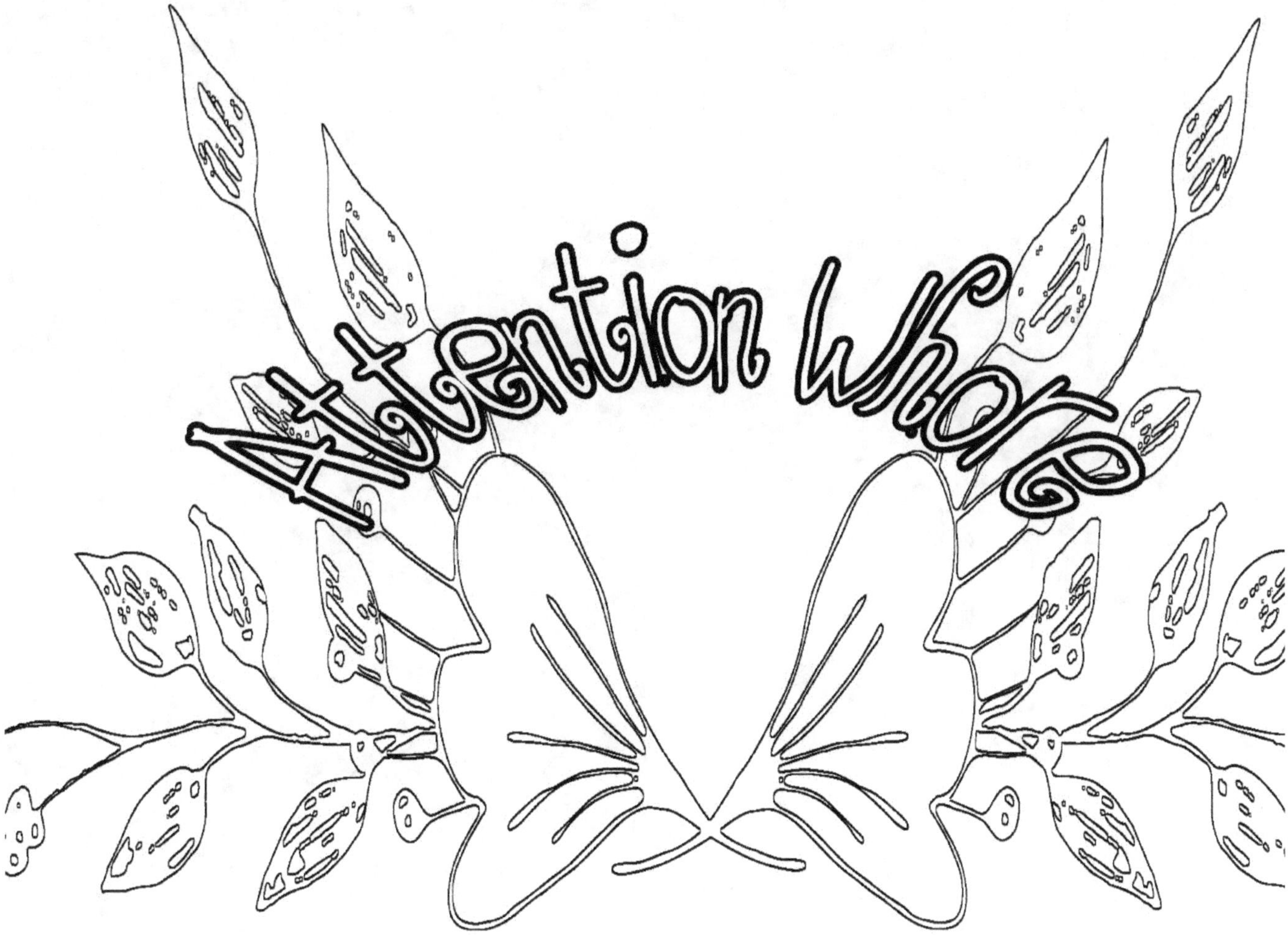
Attention Whore

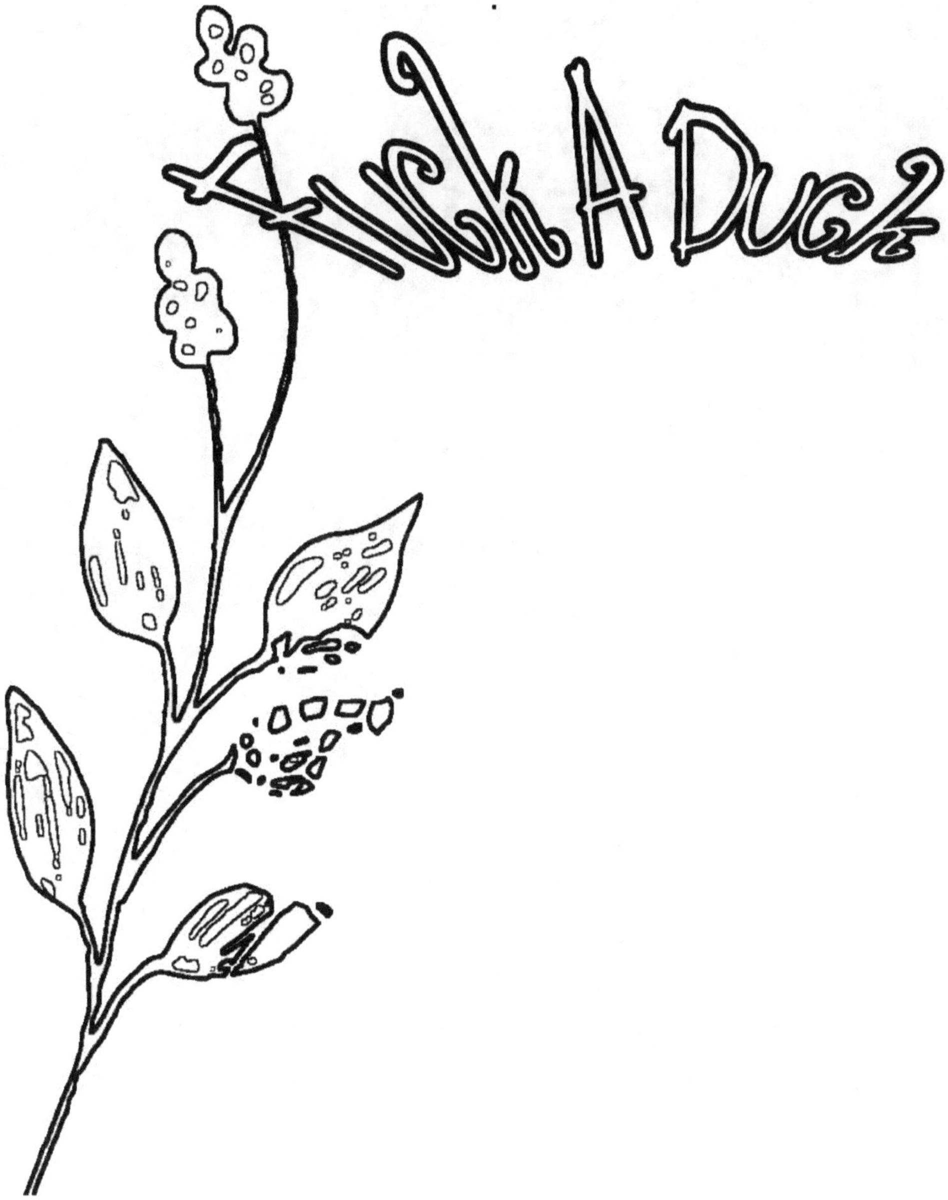
Fuck A Duck

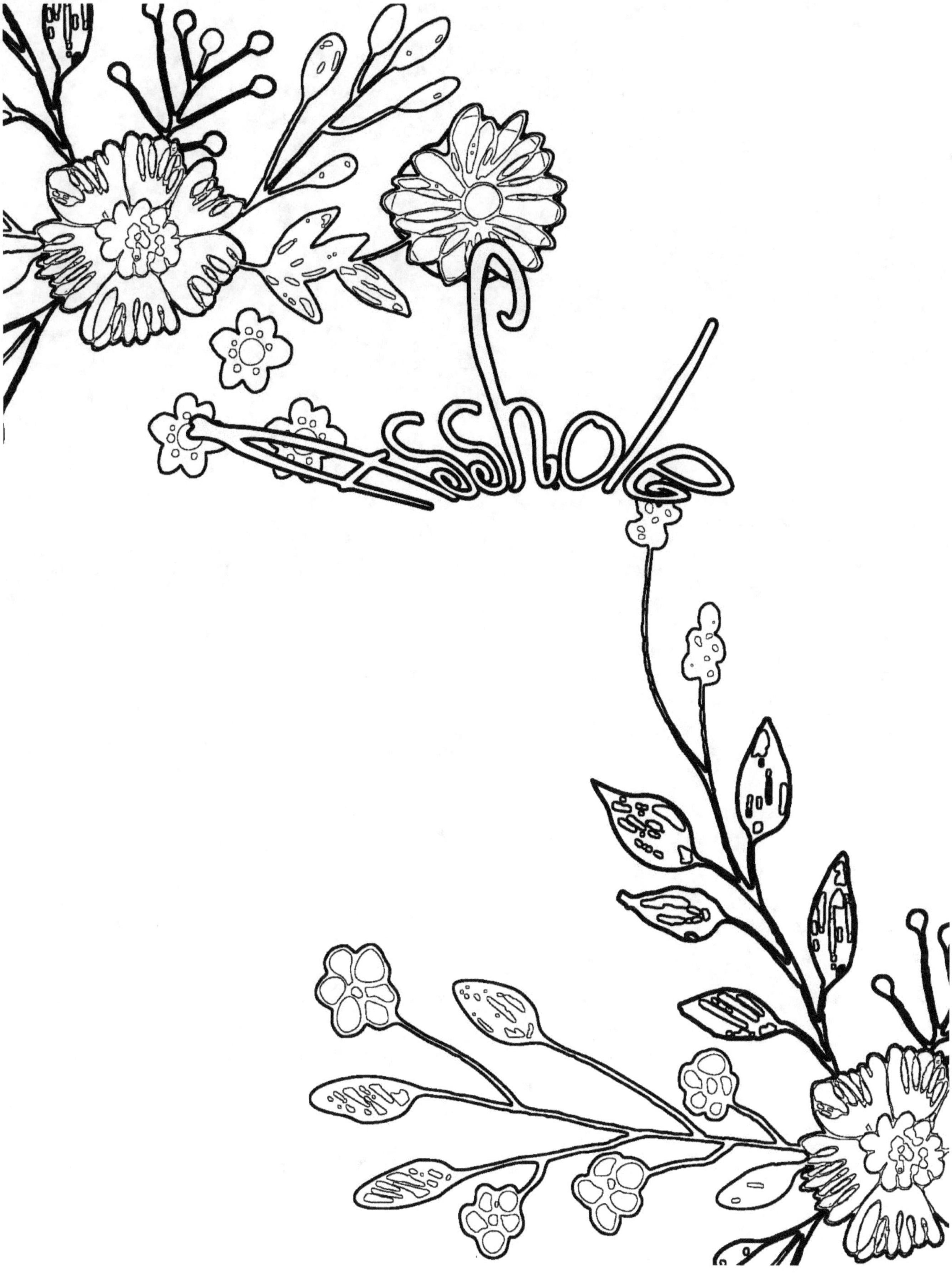
Asshole

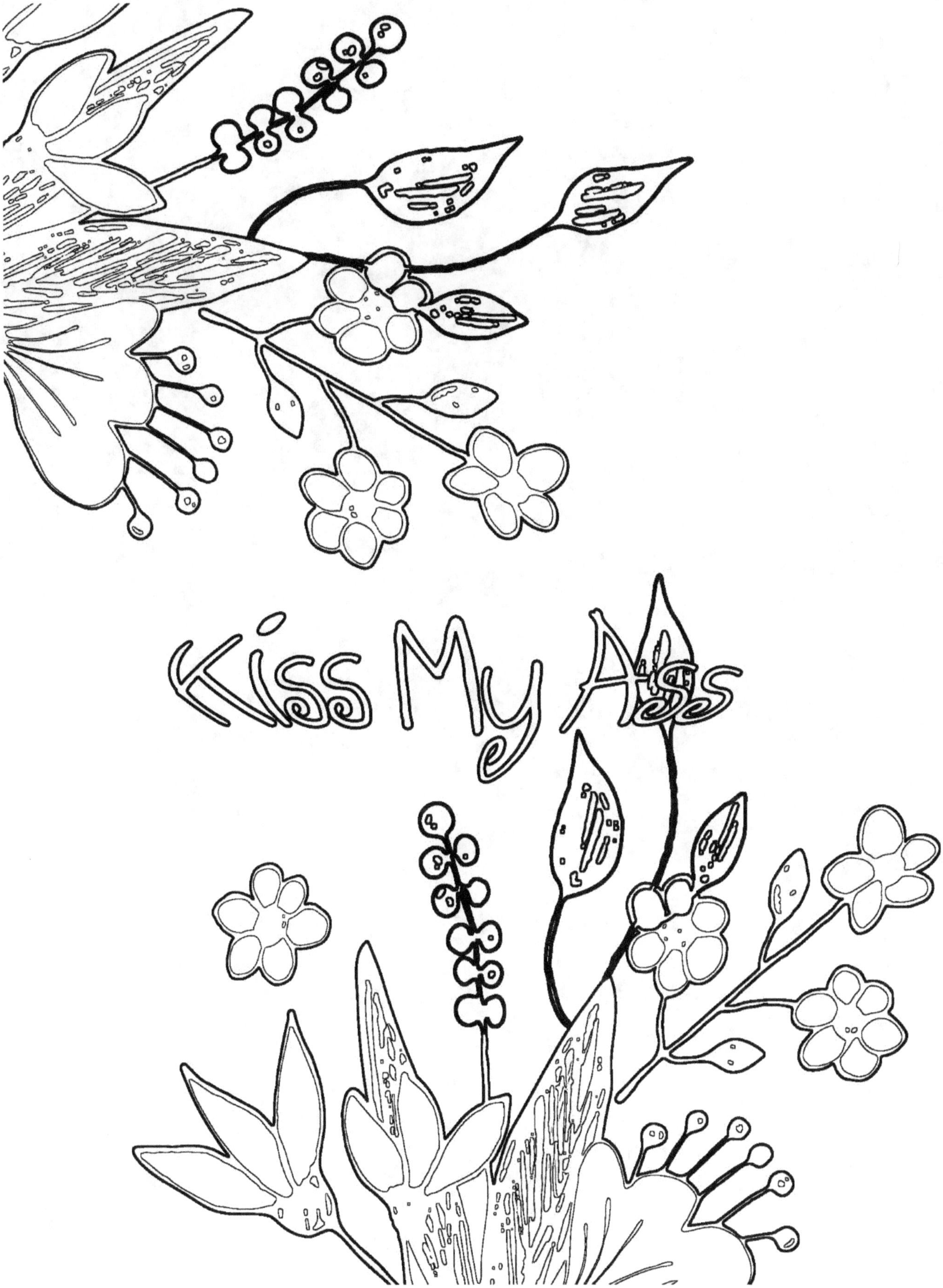
Kiss My Ass

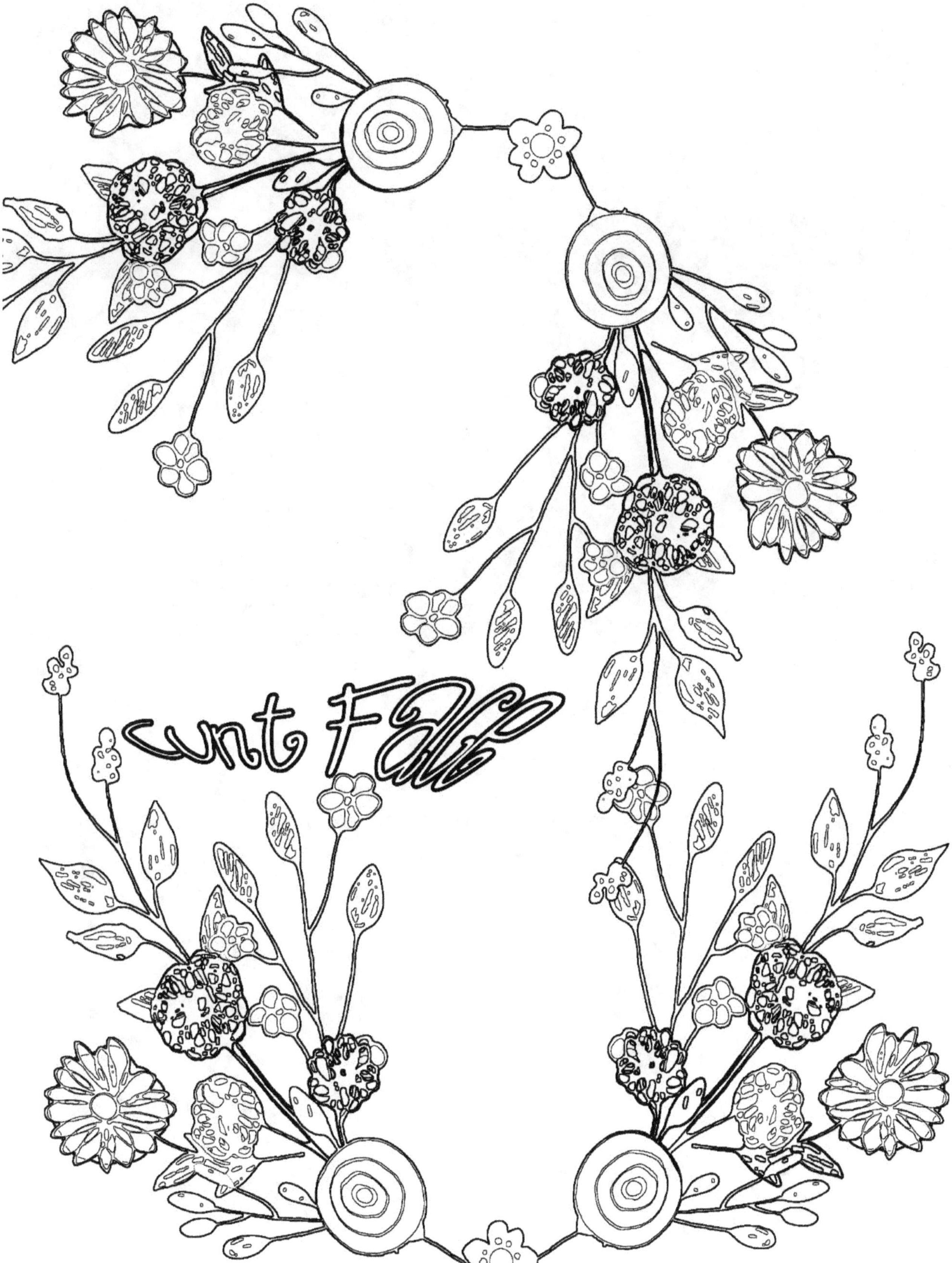
cunt Face

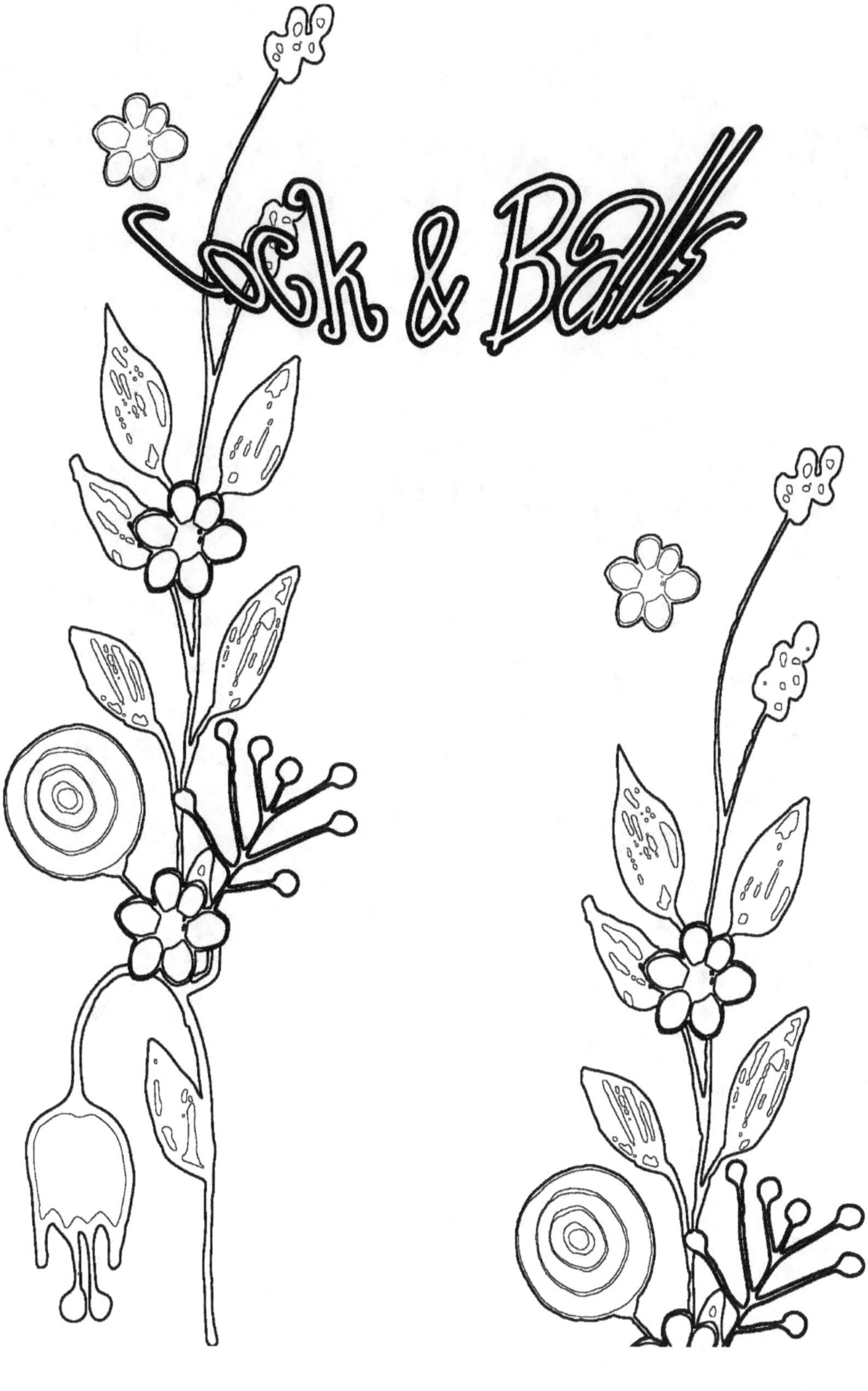
Cock & Balls

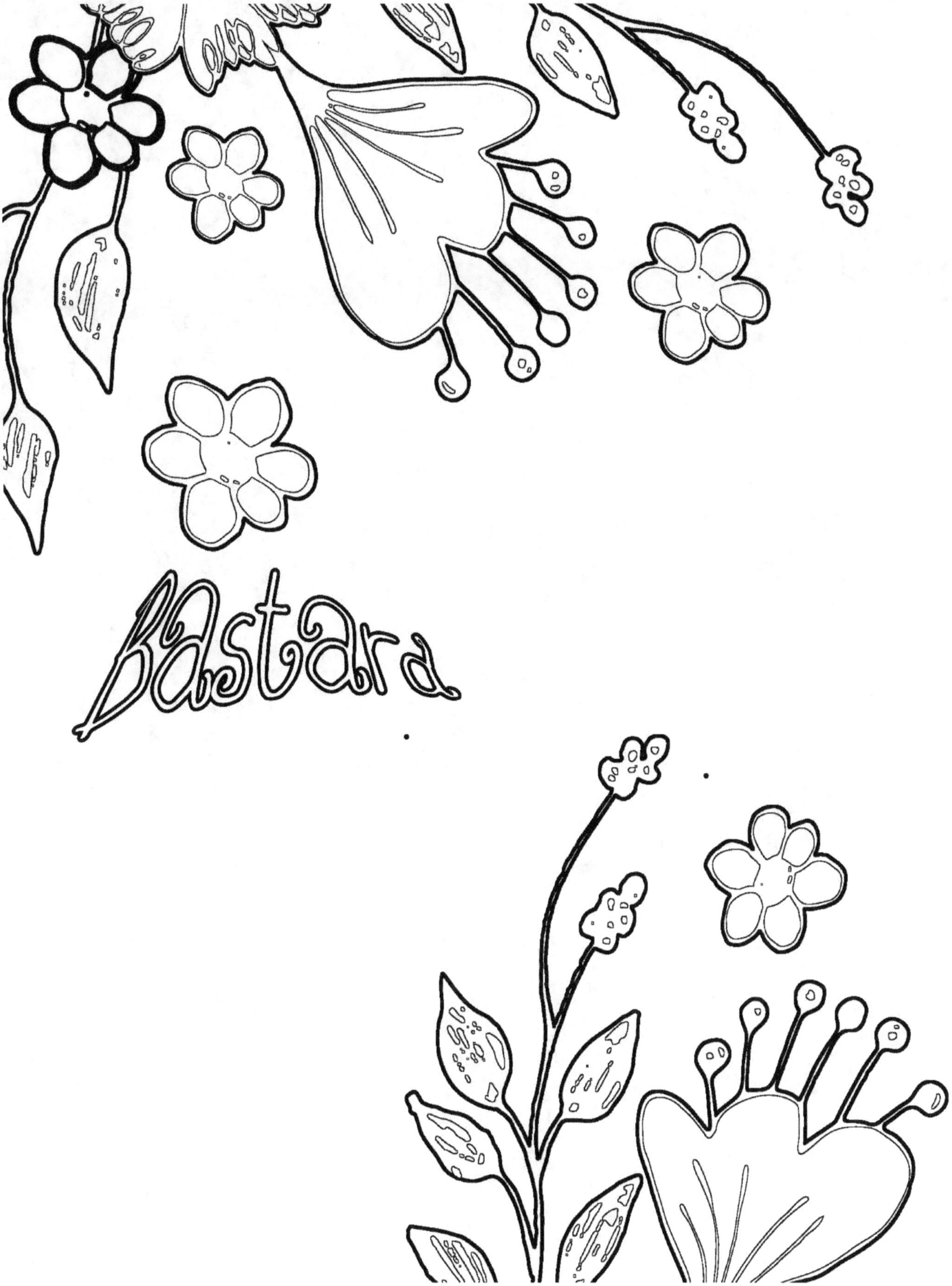
Bastara

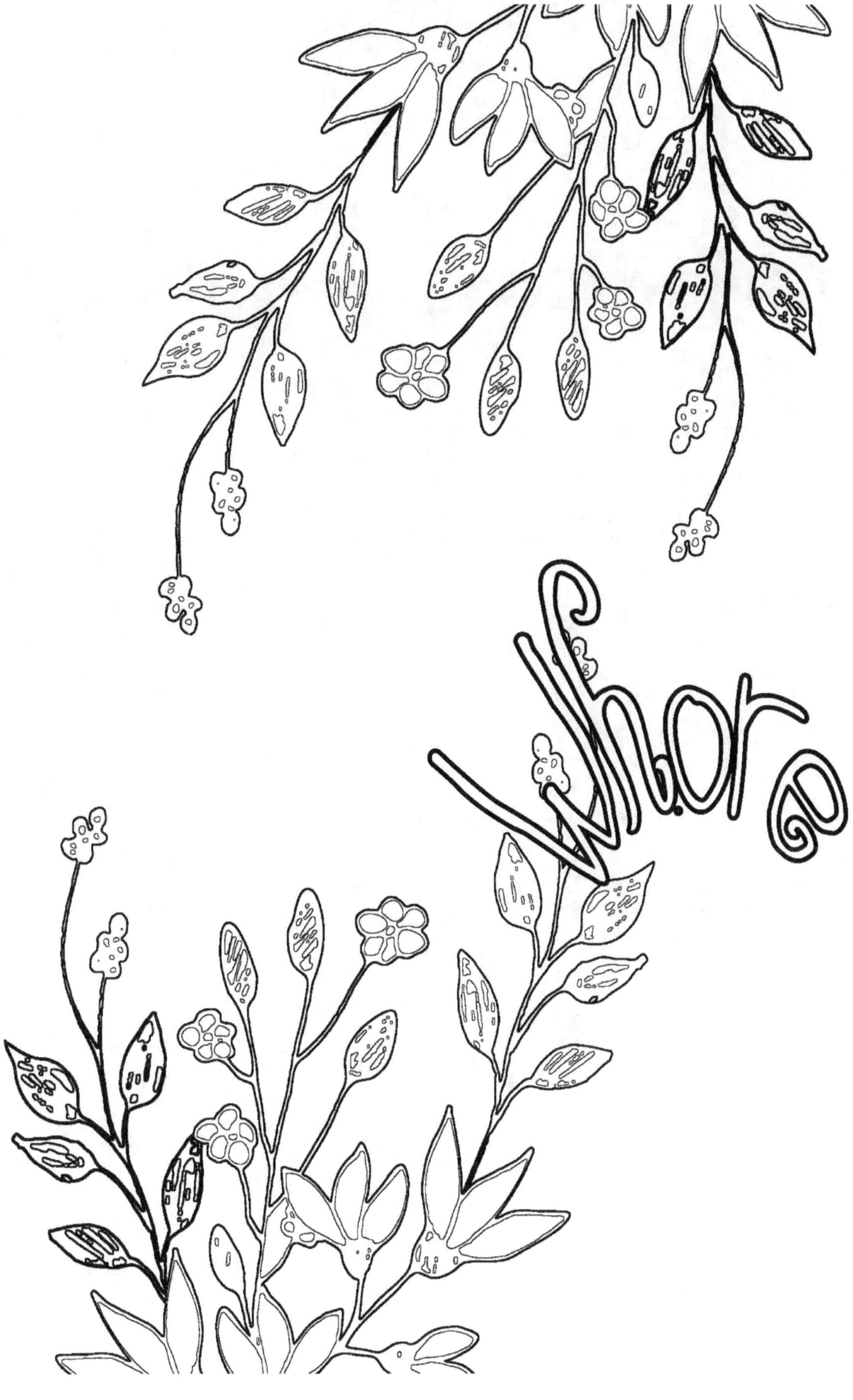
Whore

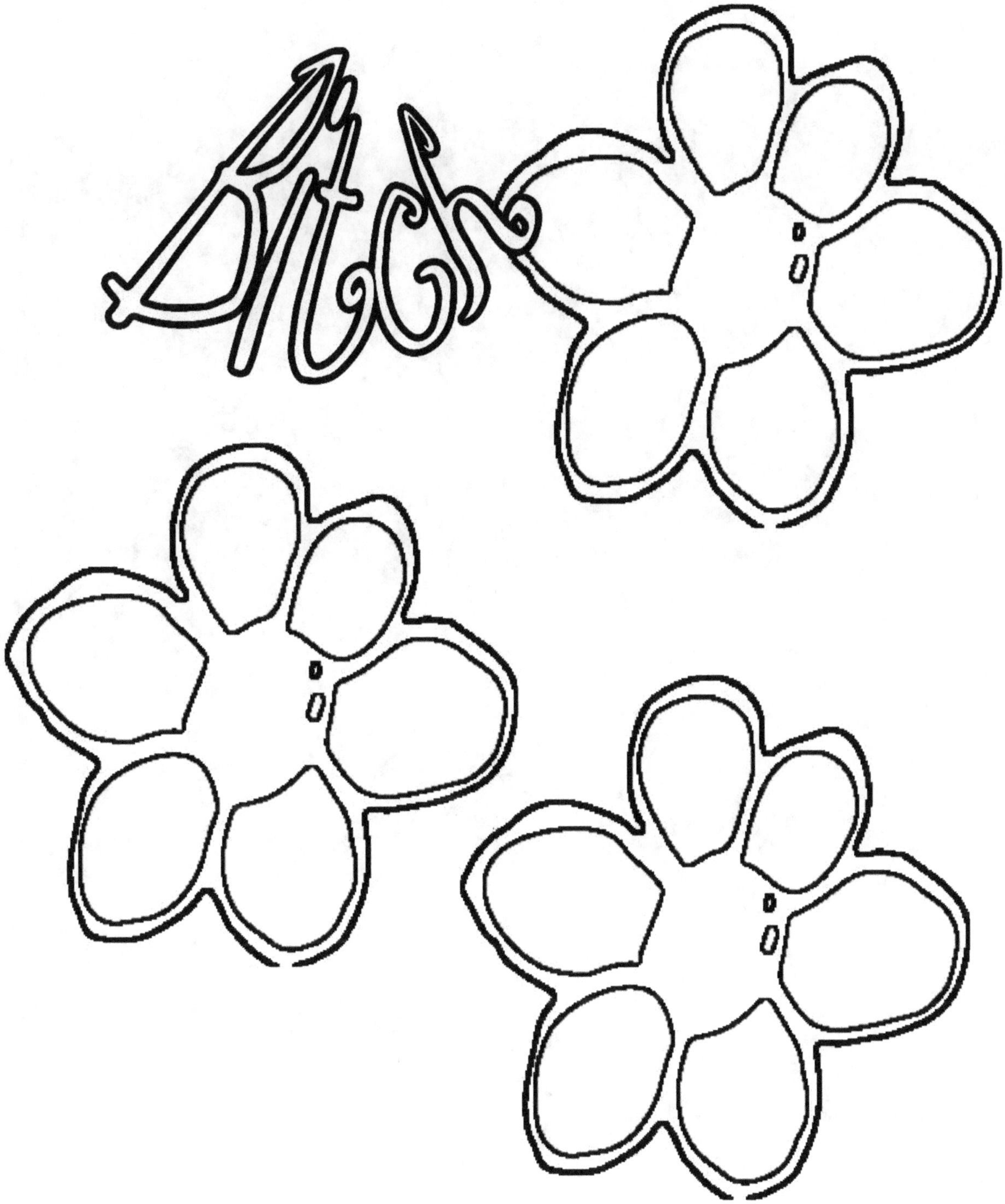
Bitch

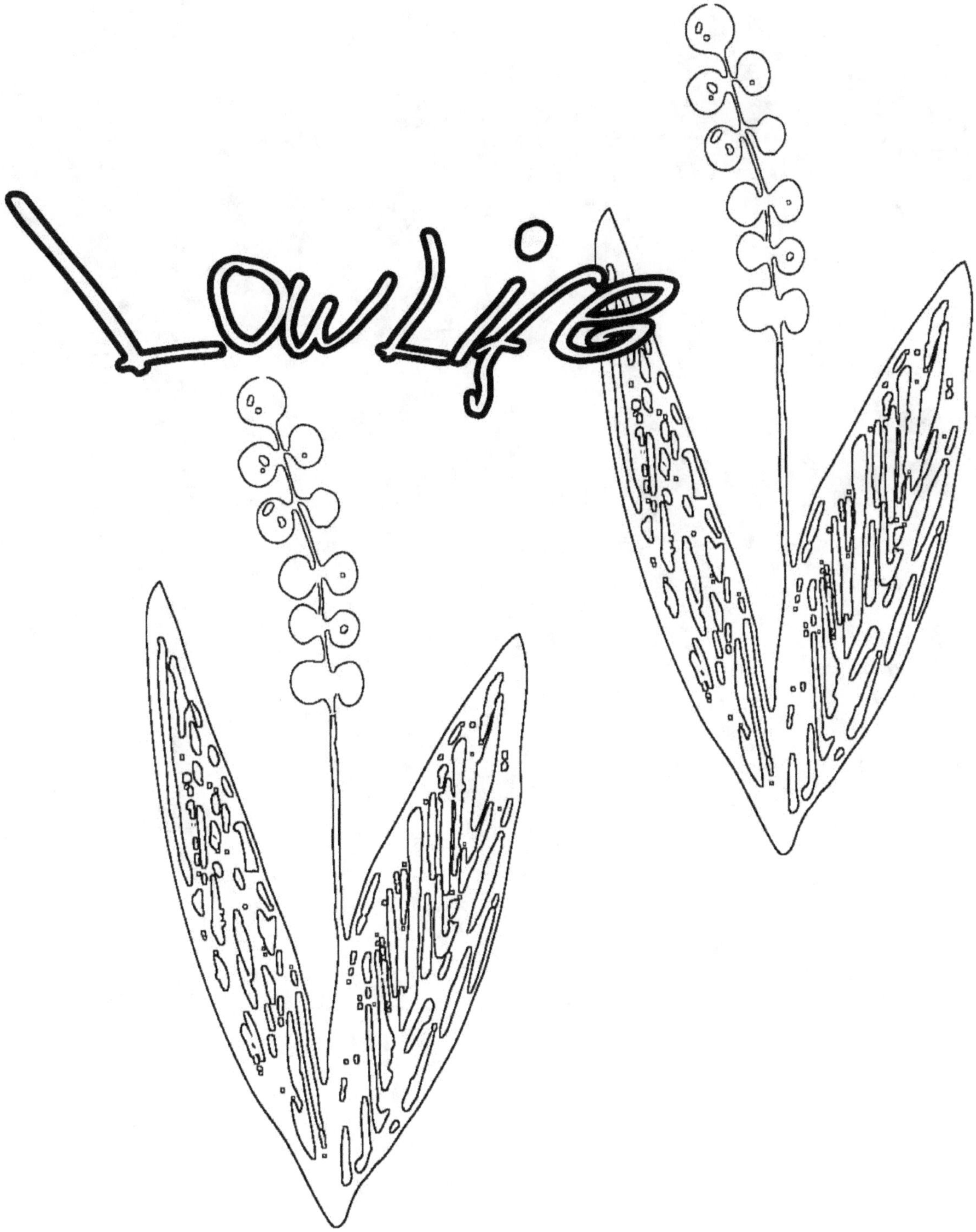
LowLife

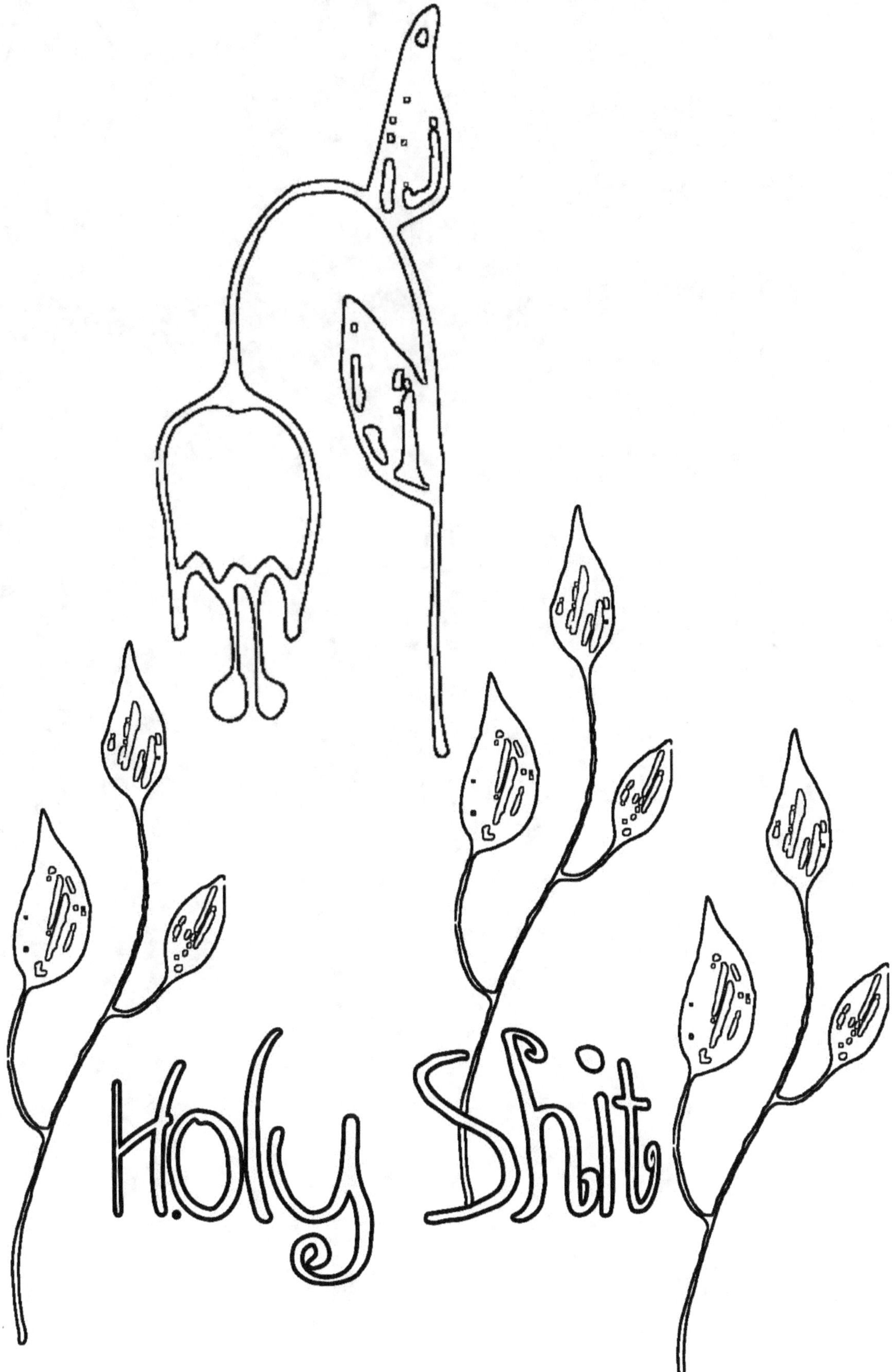
Holy Shit

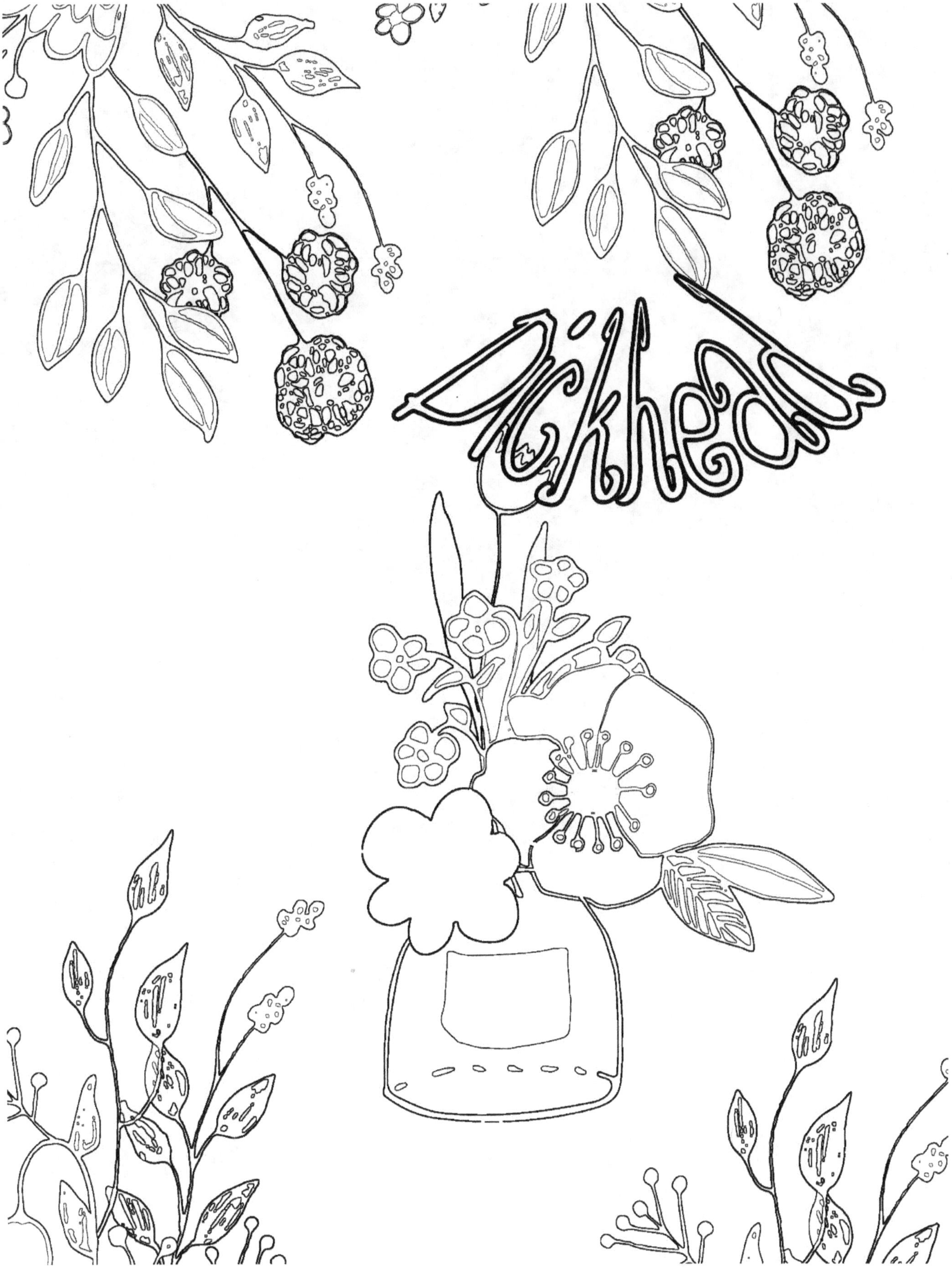
Dickhead

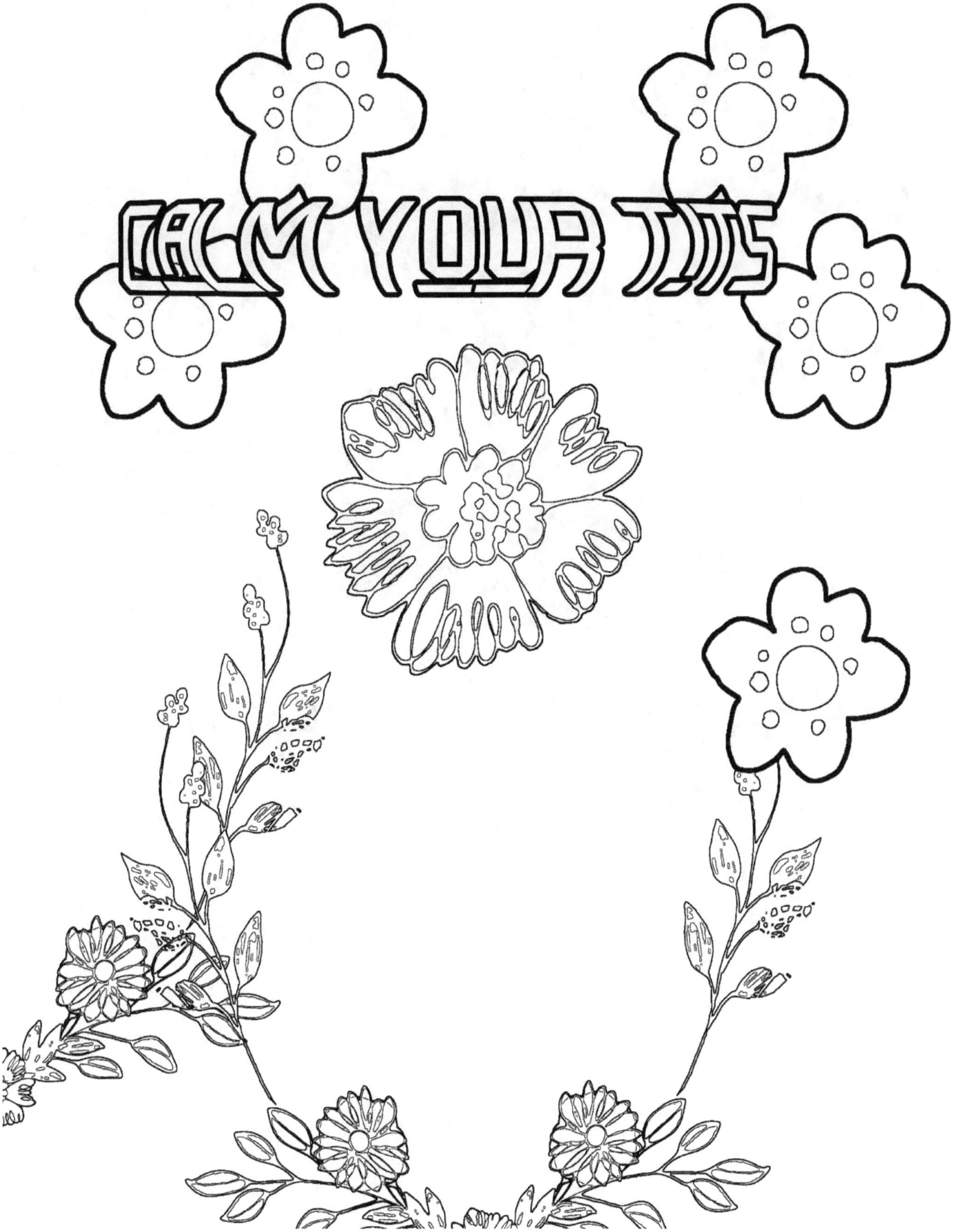
CALM YOUR TITS

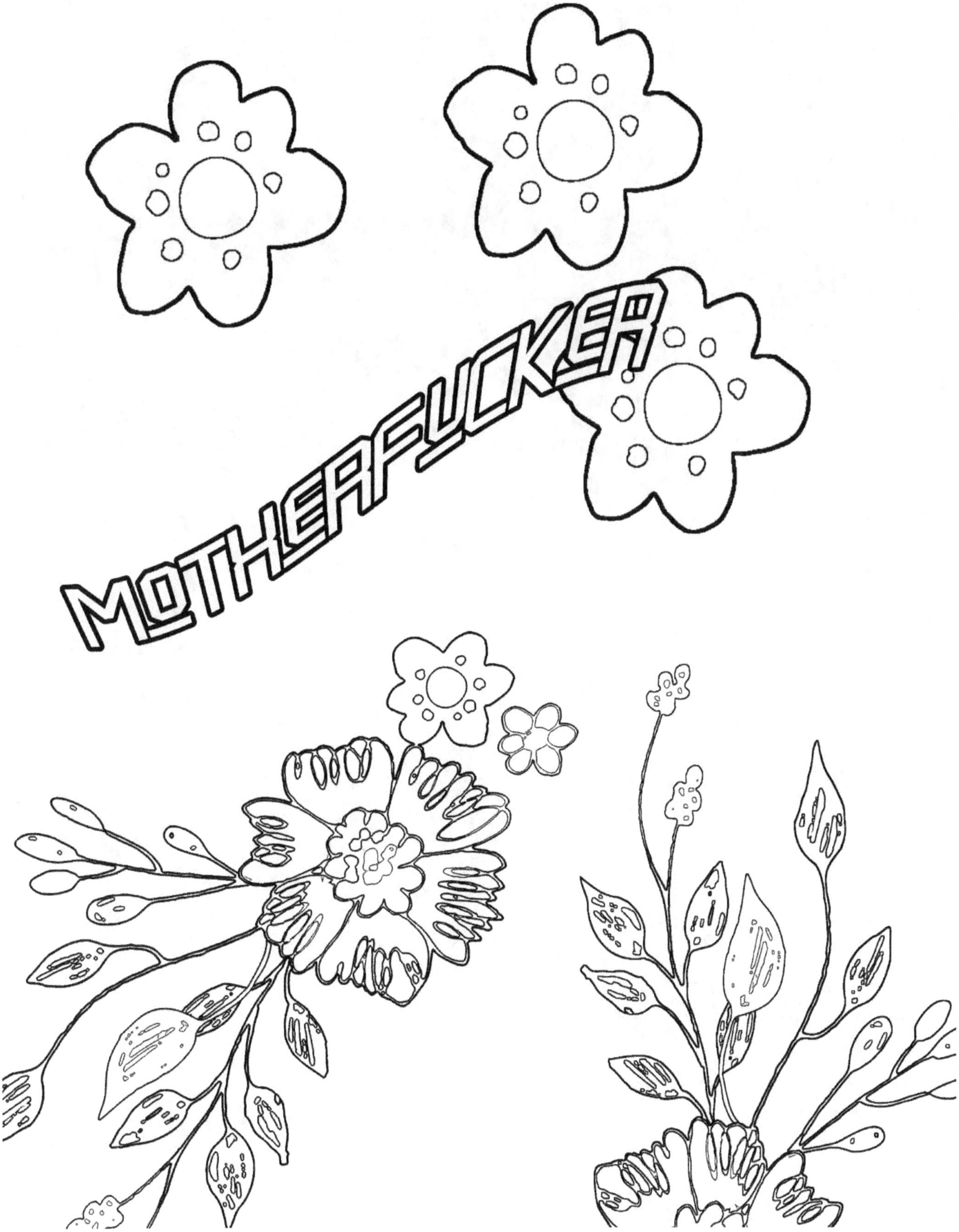
MOTHERFUCKER

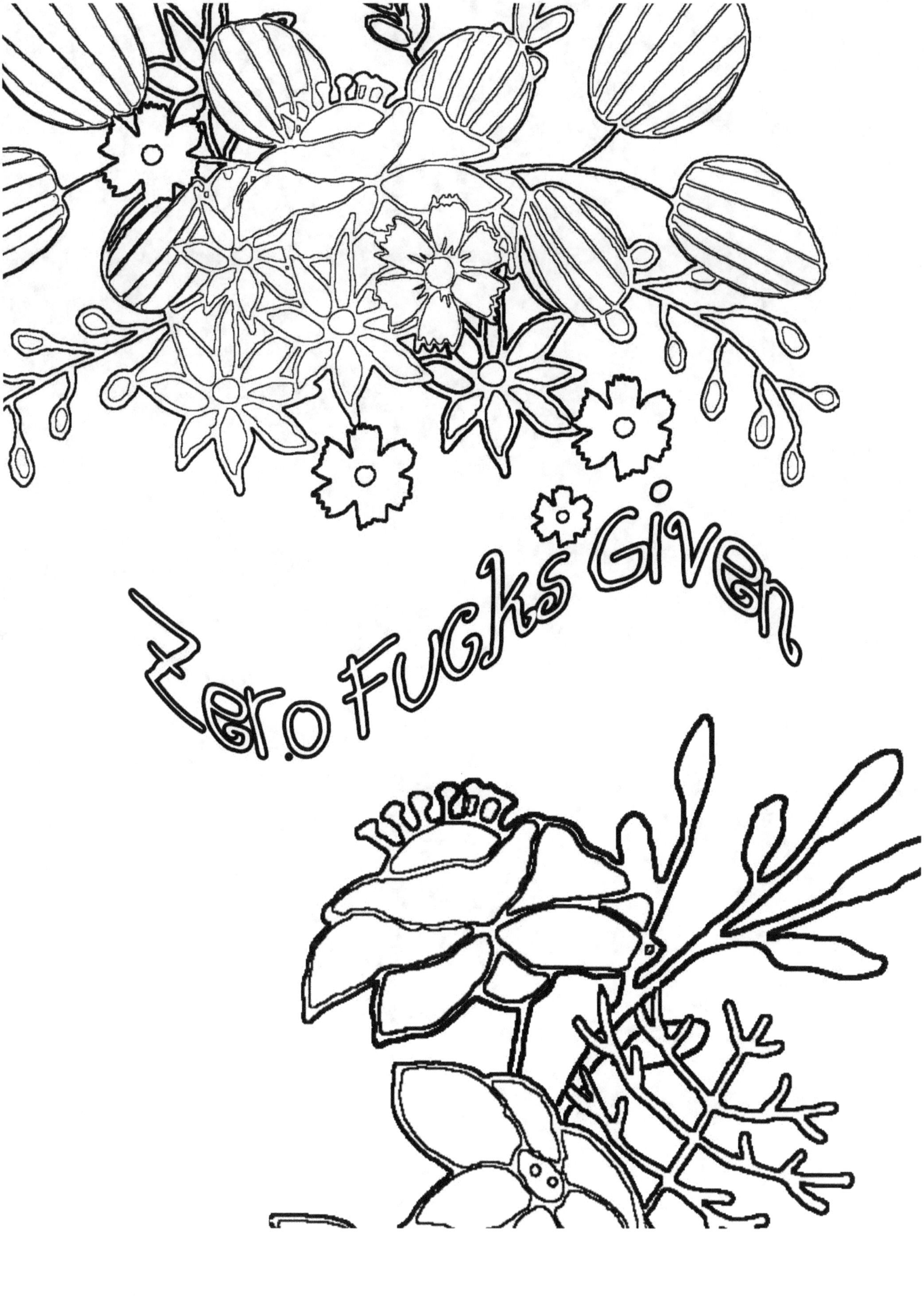
Zero Fucks Given

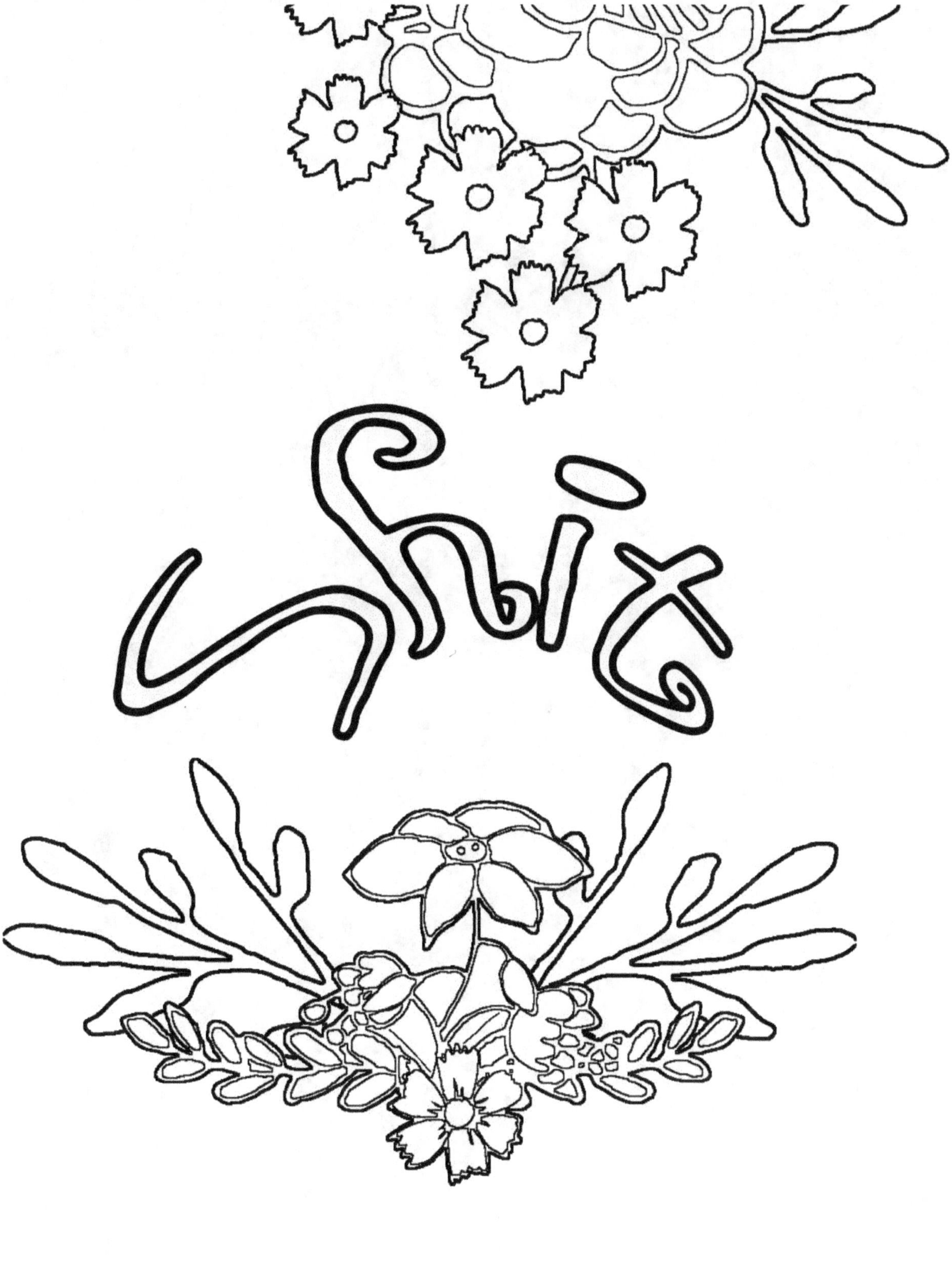
Shit

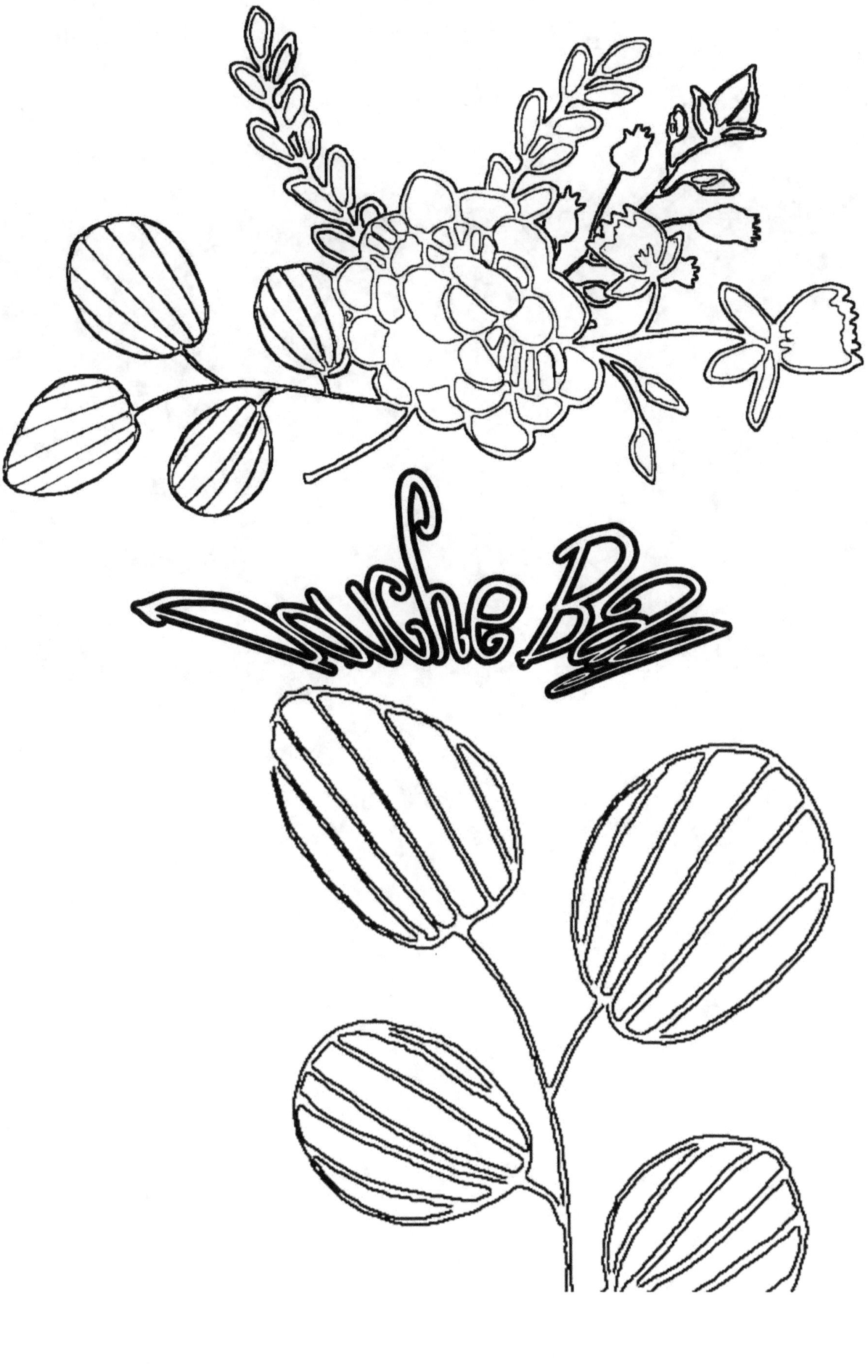
Douche Bag

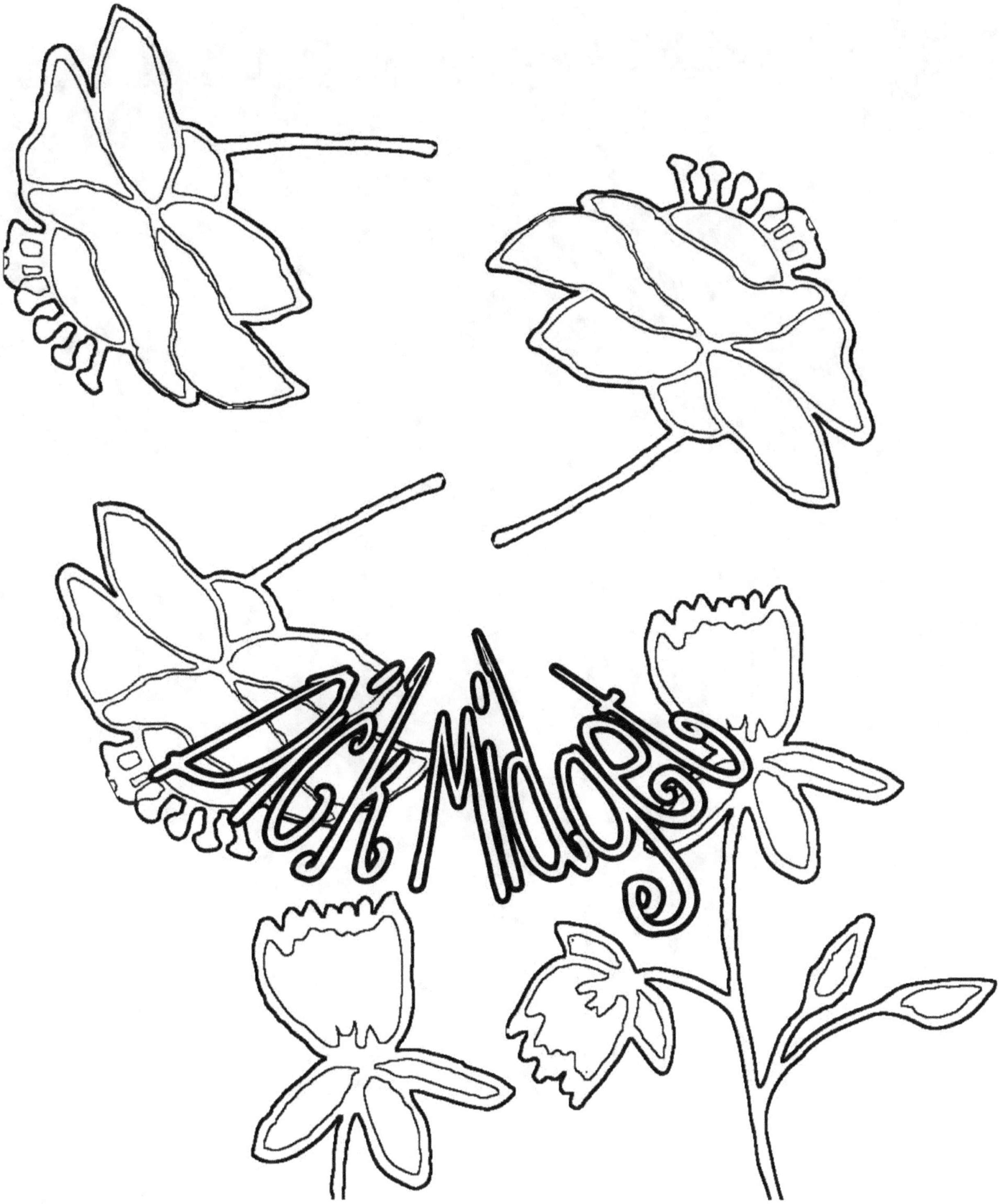
Dick Midget

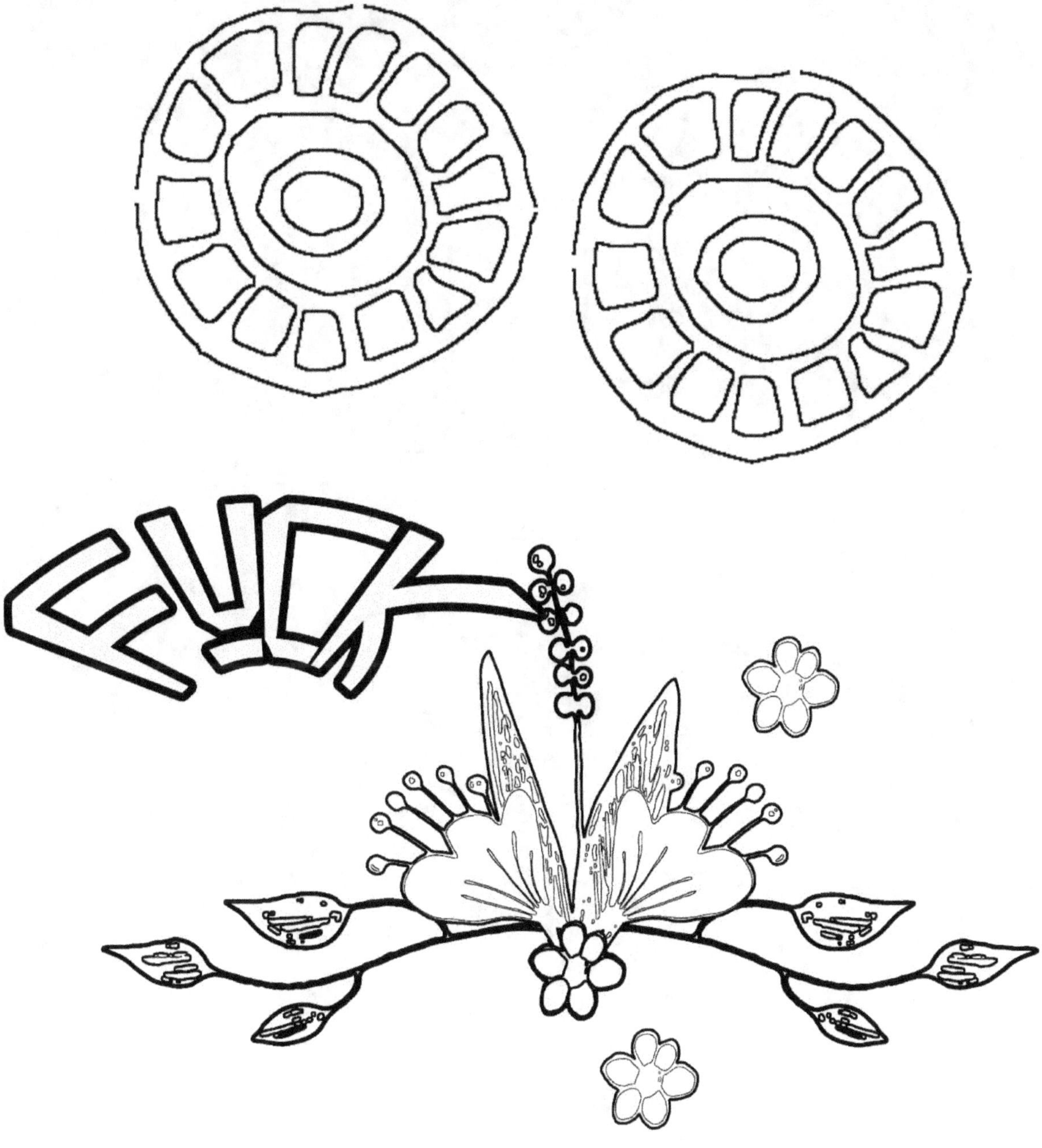
FUCK

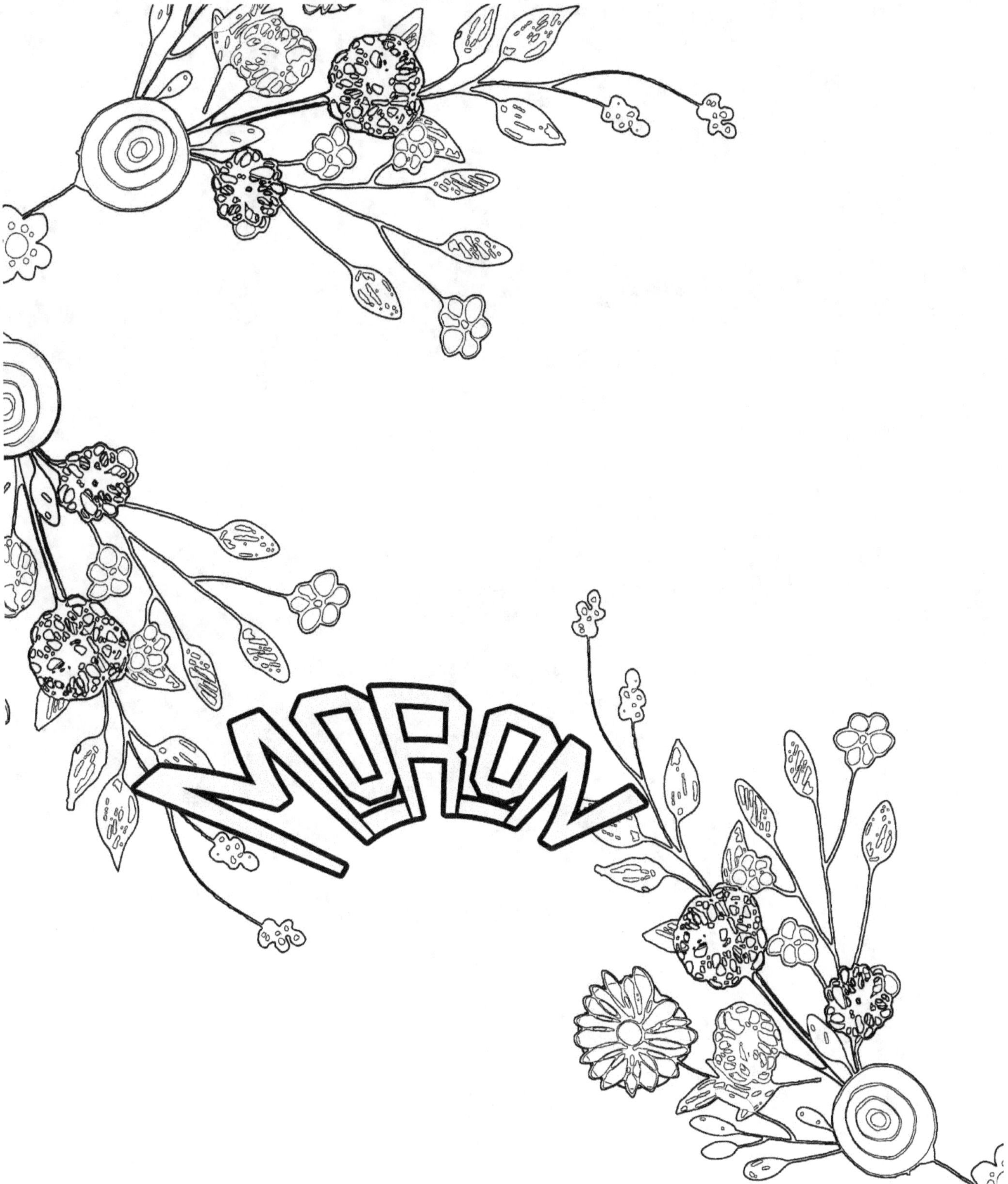
MORON

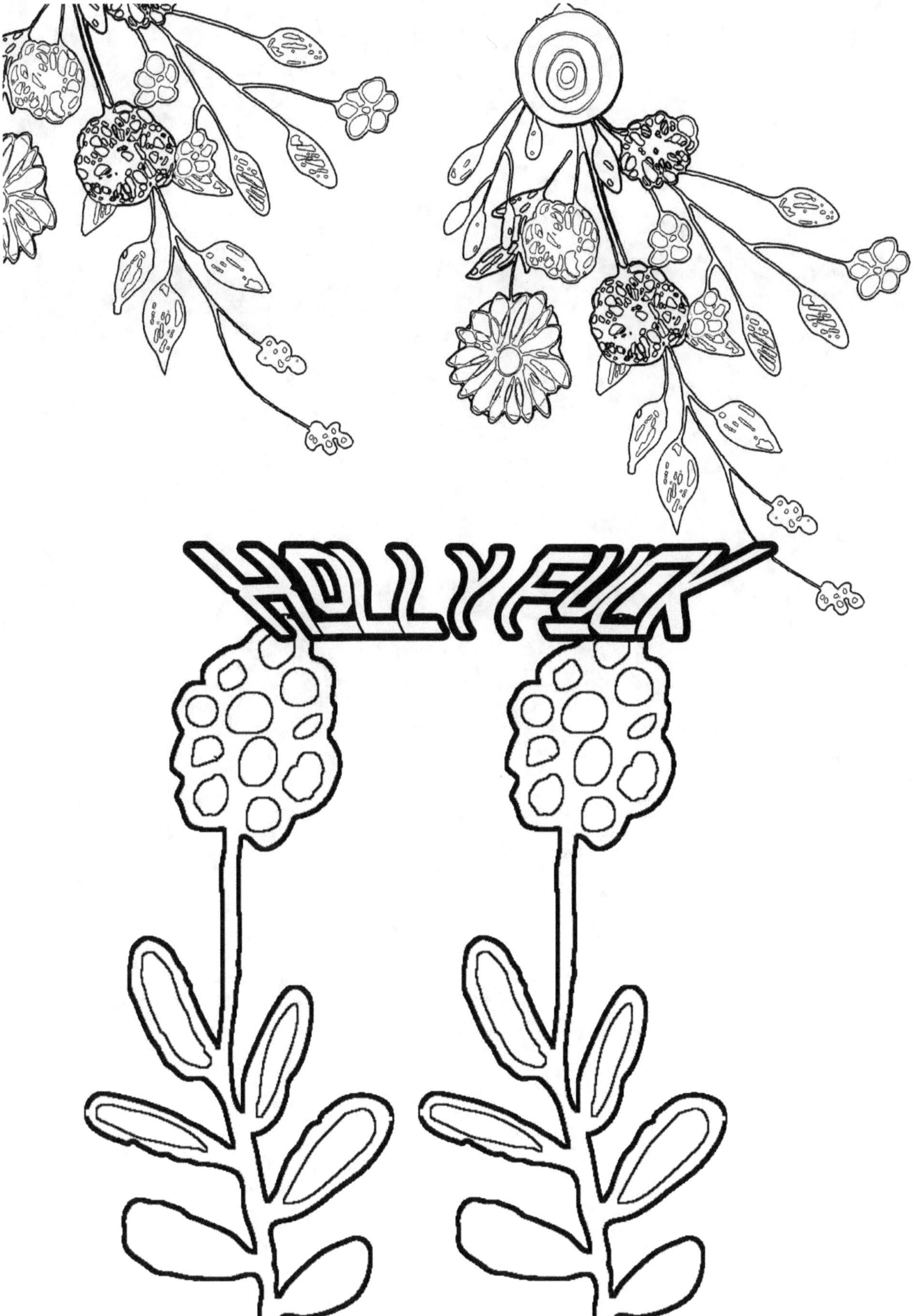
HOLLY FUCK

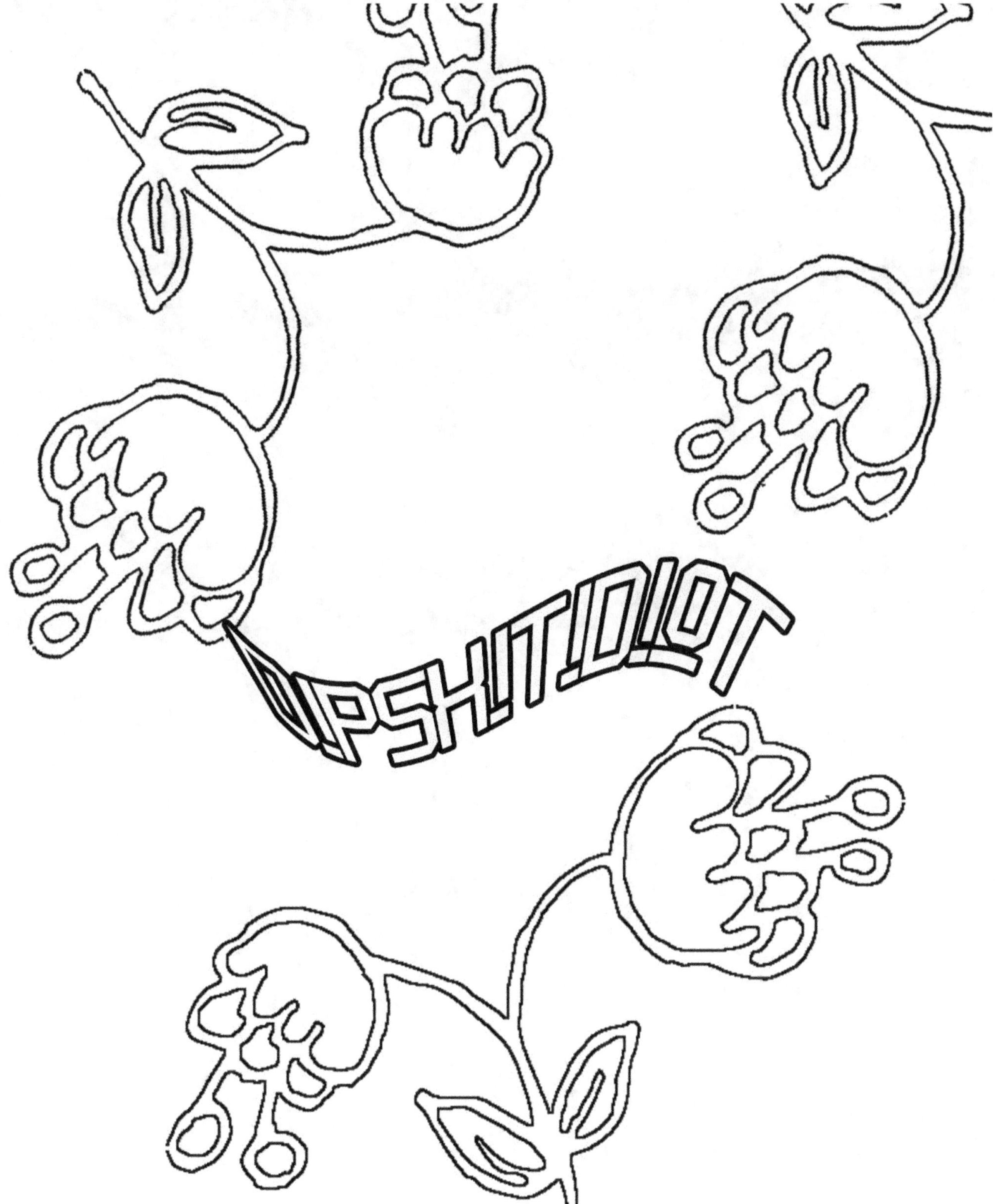
DIPSHIT IDIOT

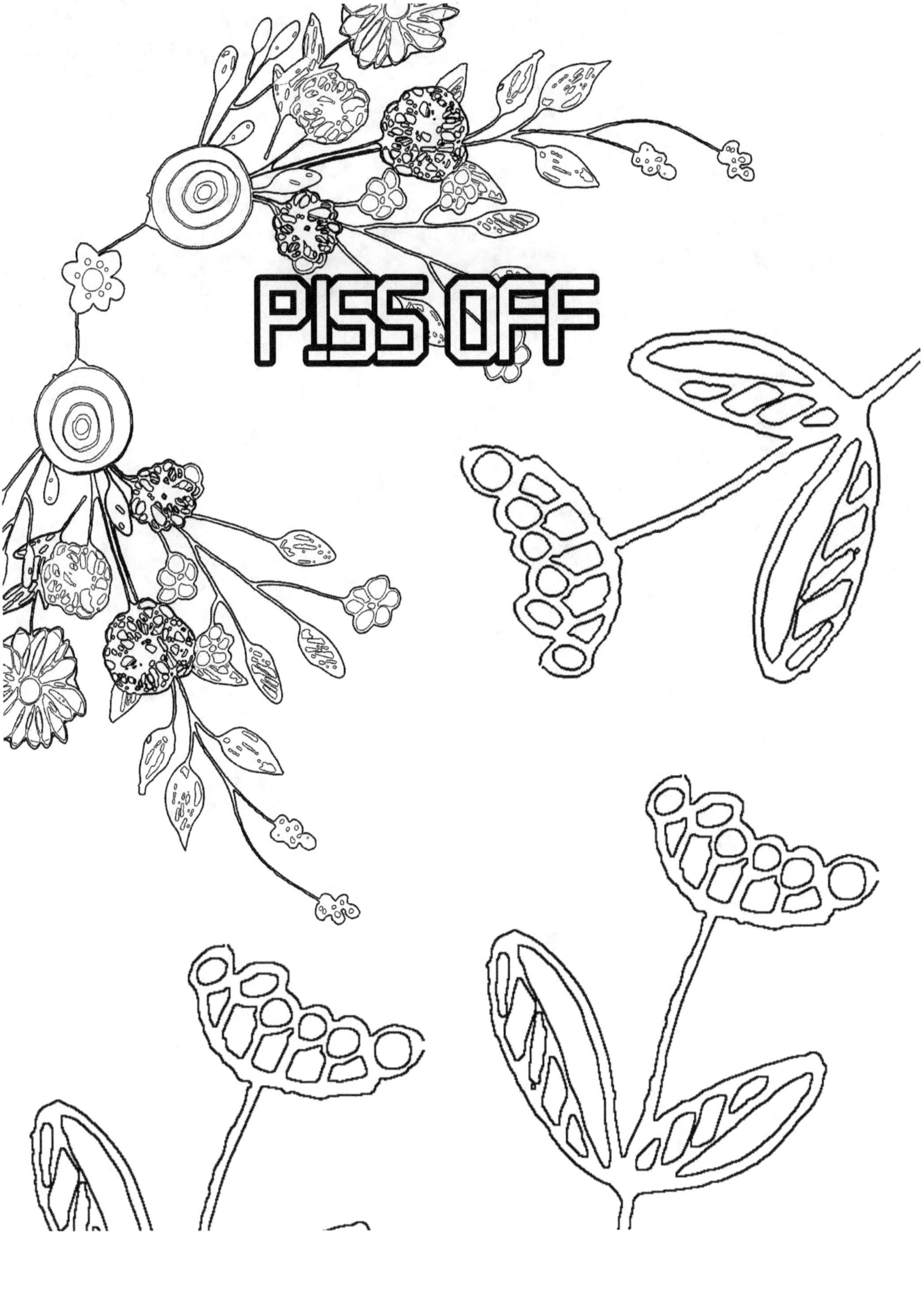
PISS OFF

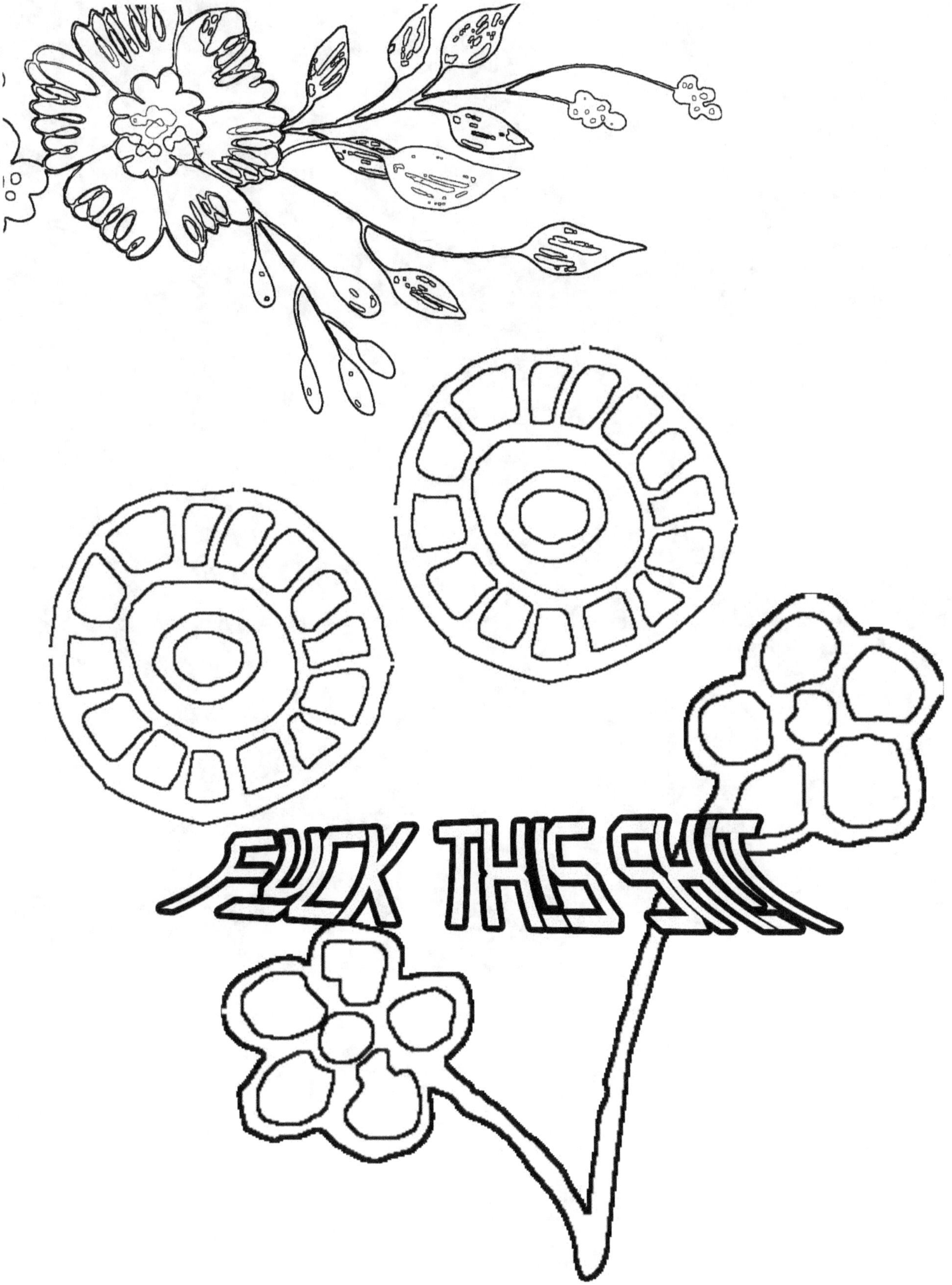
FUCK THIS SHIT

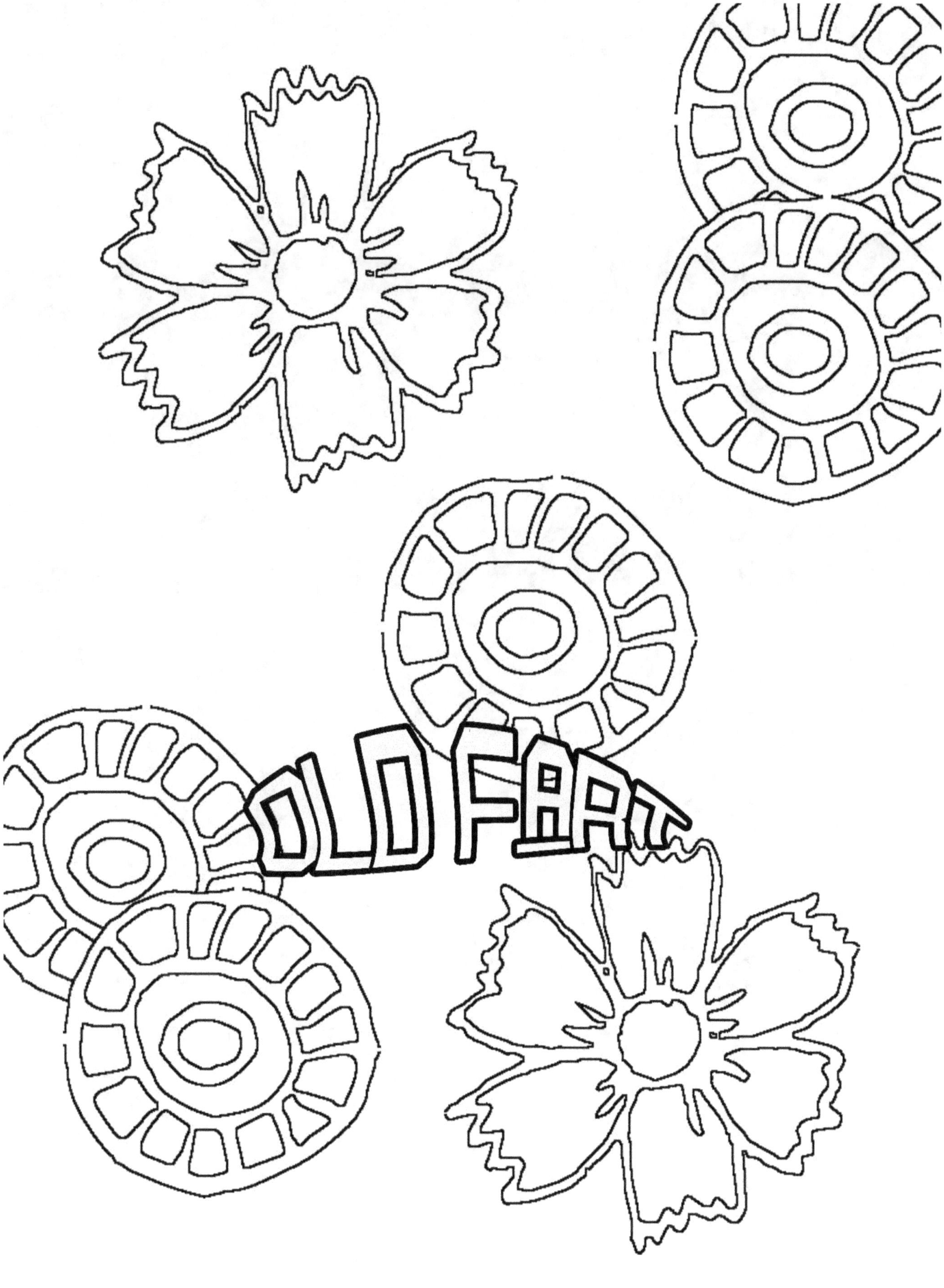
OLD FART

www.ingramcontent.com/pod-product-compliance
Lightning Source LLC
Chambersburg PA
CBHW081749170526
45167CB00009B/3970